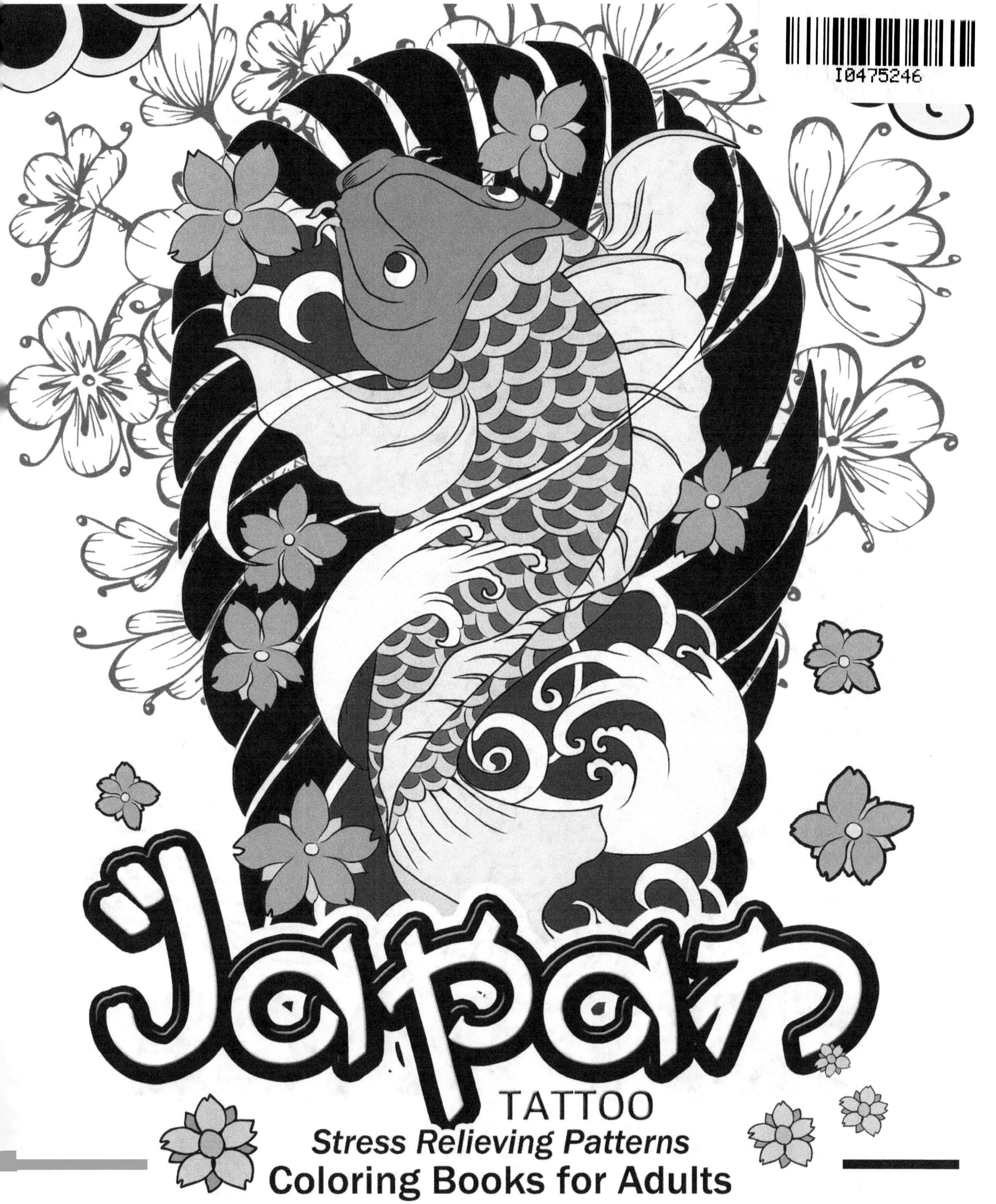

Japan

TATTOO

Stress Relieving Patterns

Coloring Books for Adults

COLOR

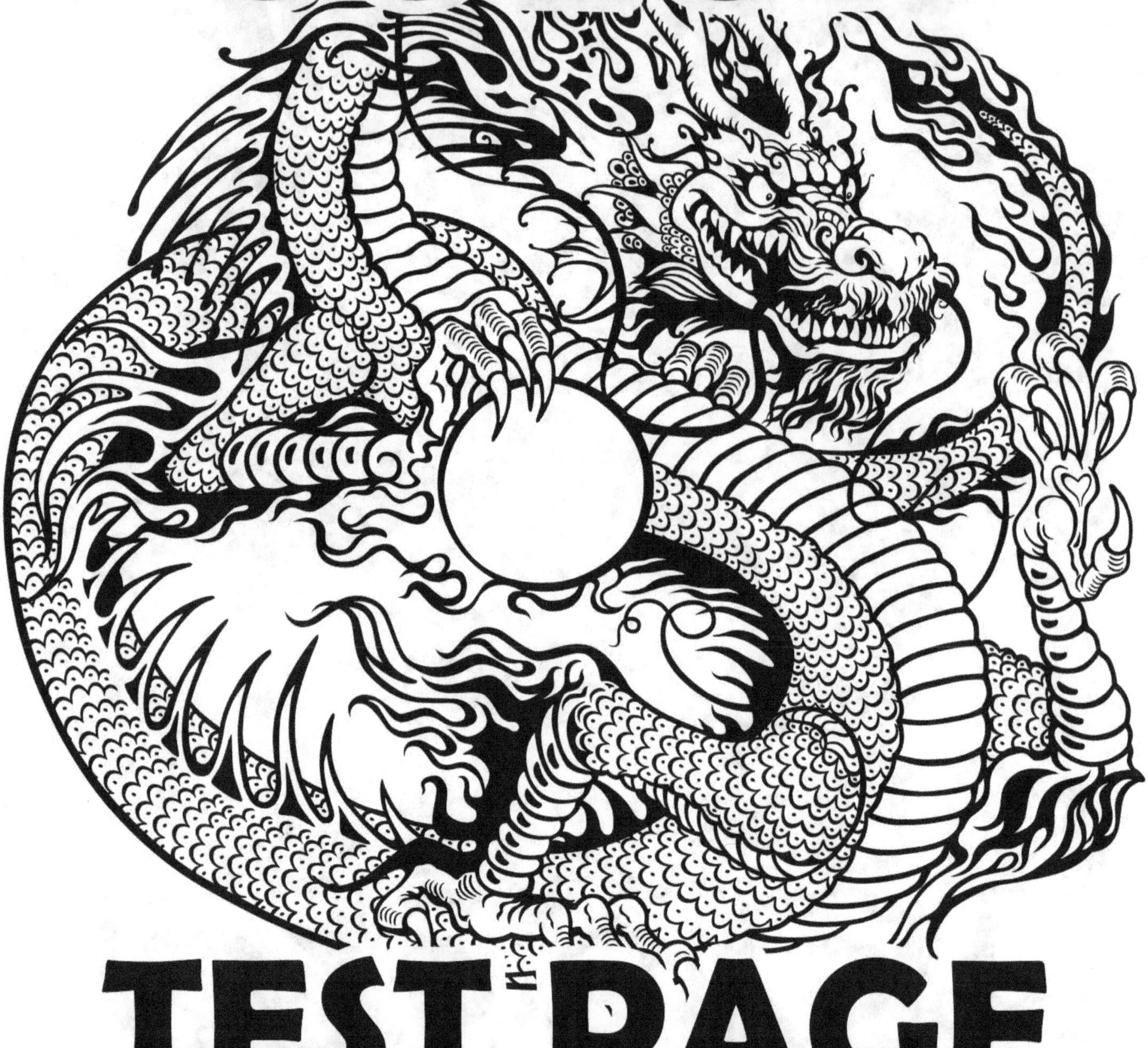

TEST PAGE

TEST YOUR COLOR

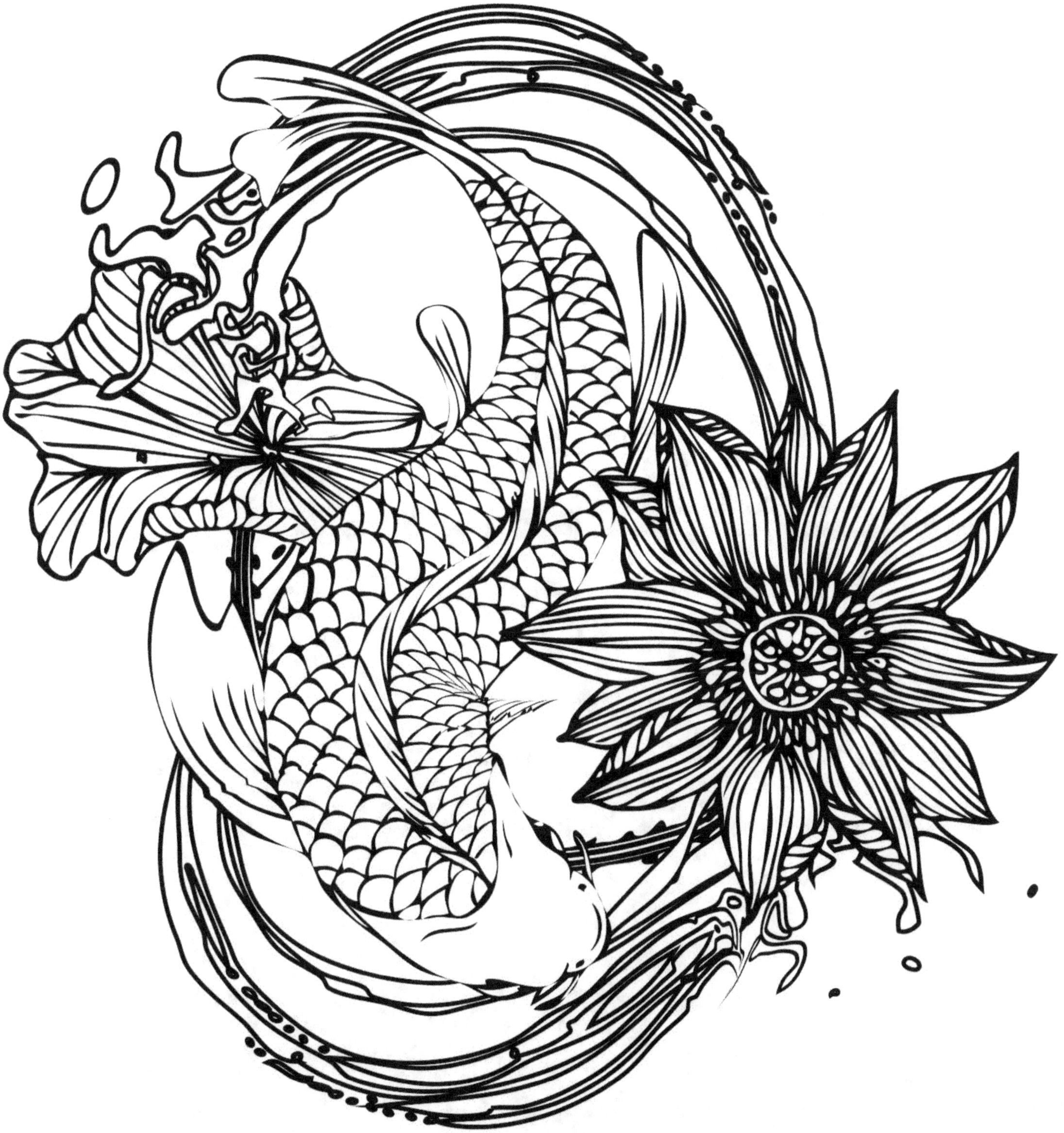

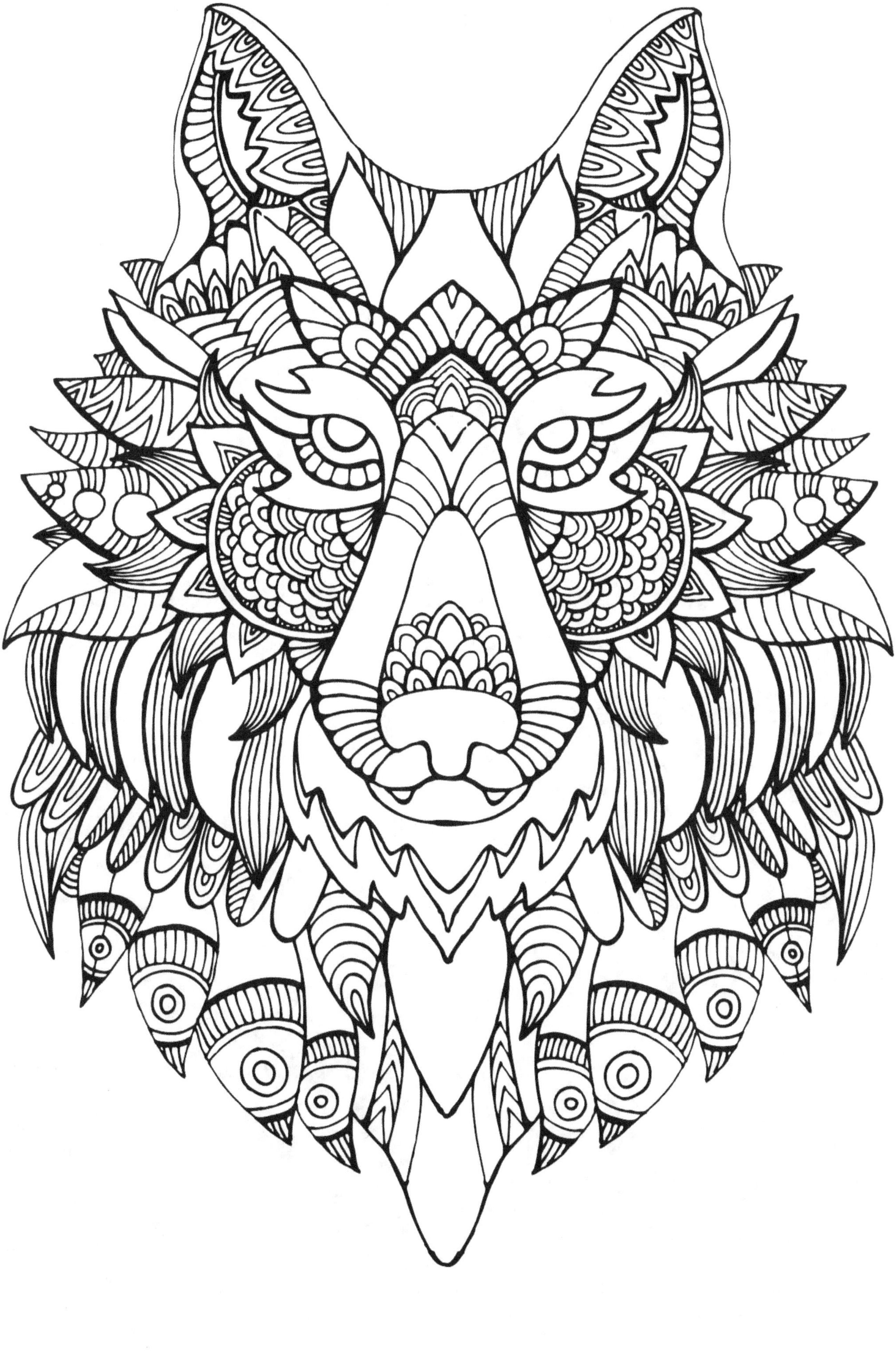

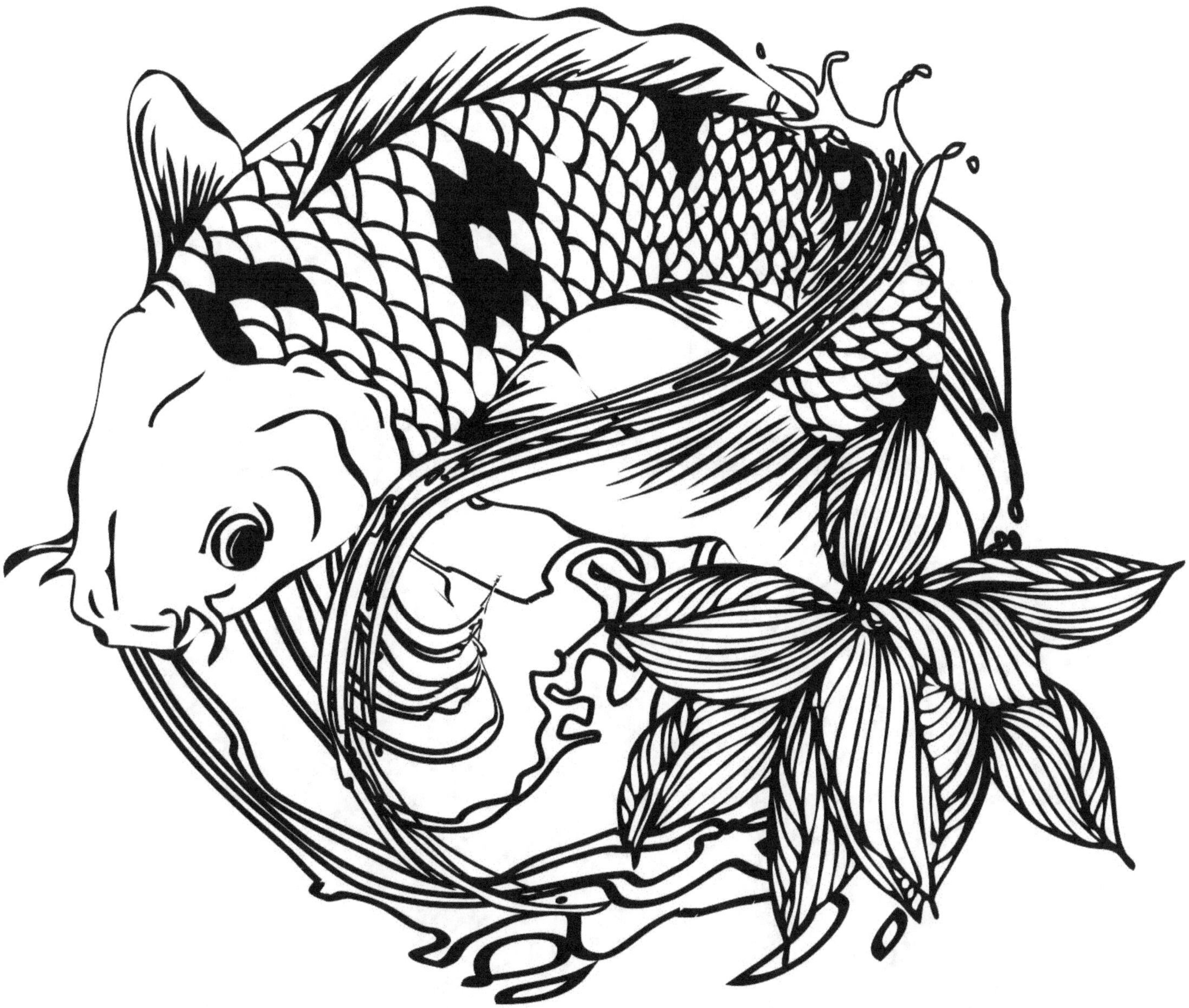

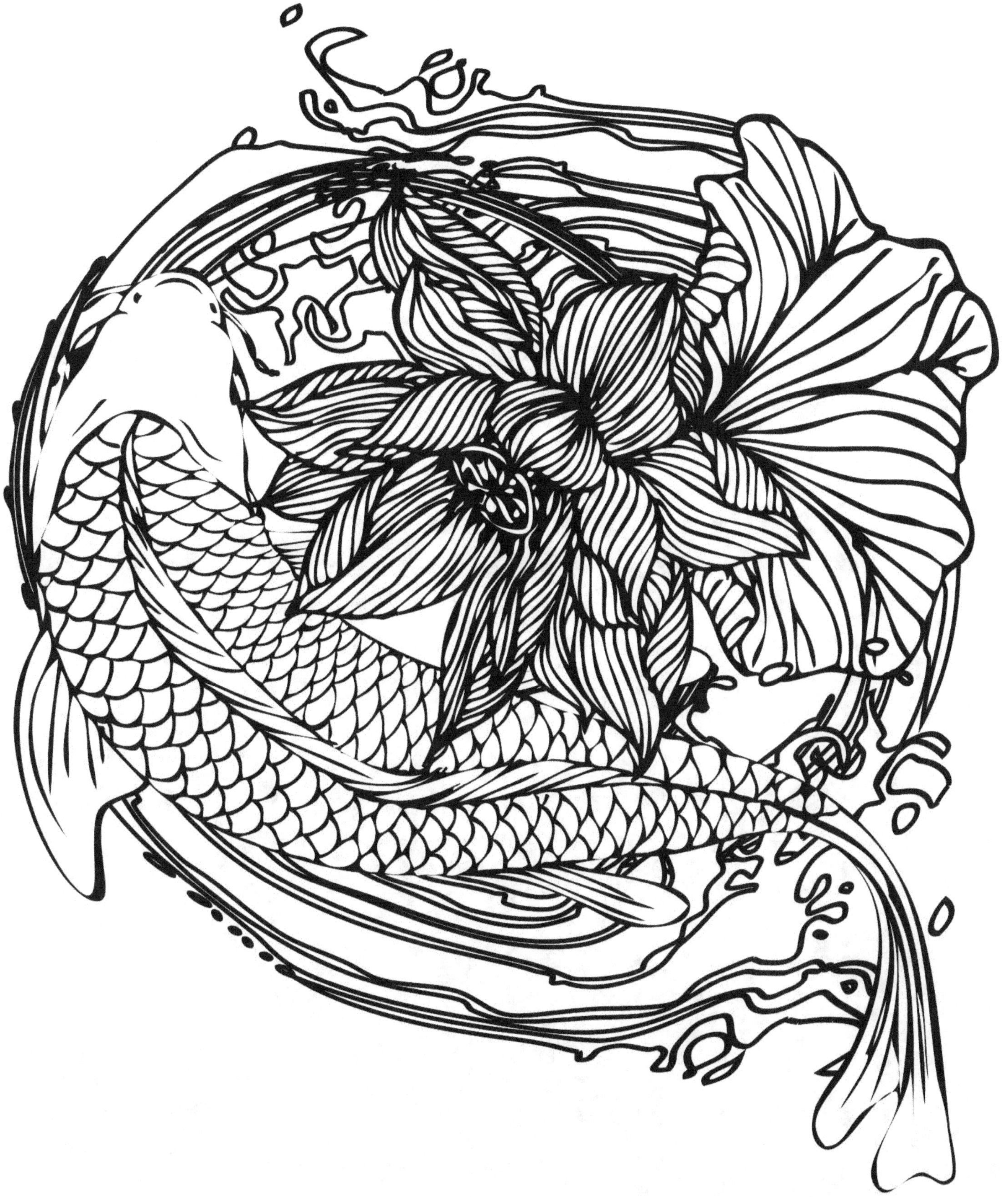

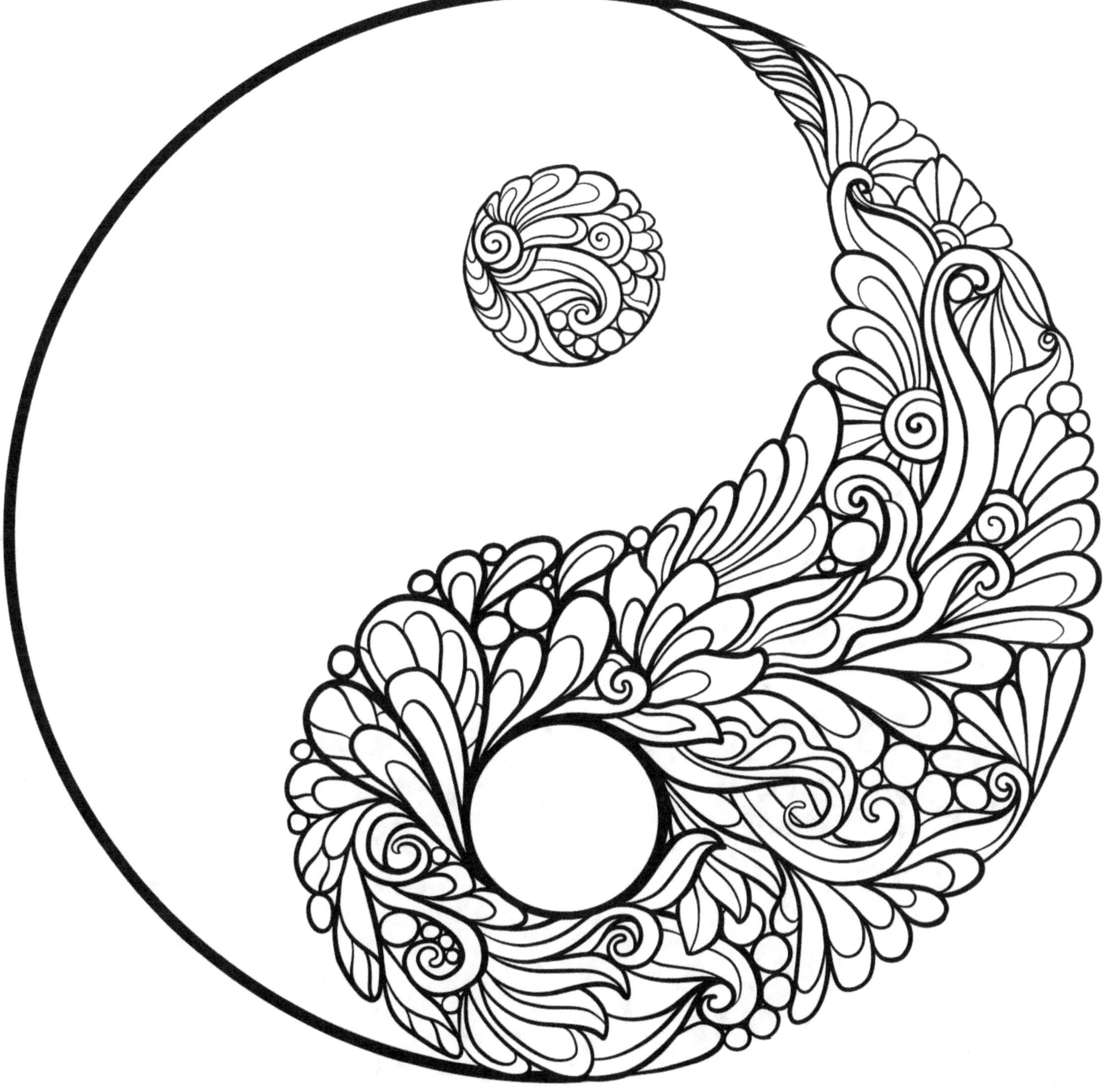

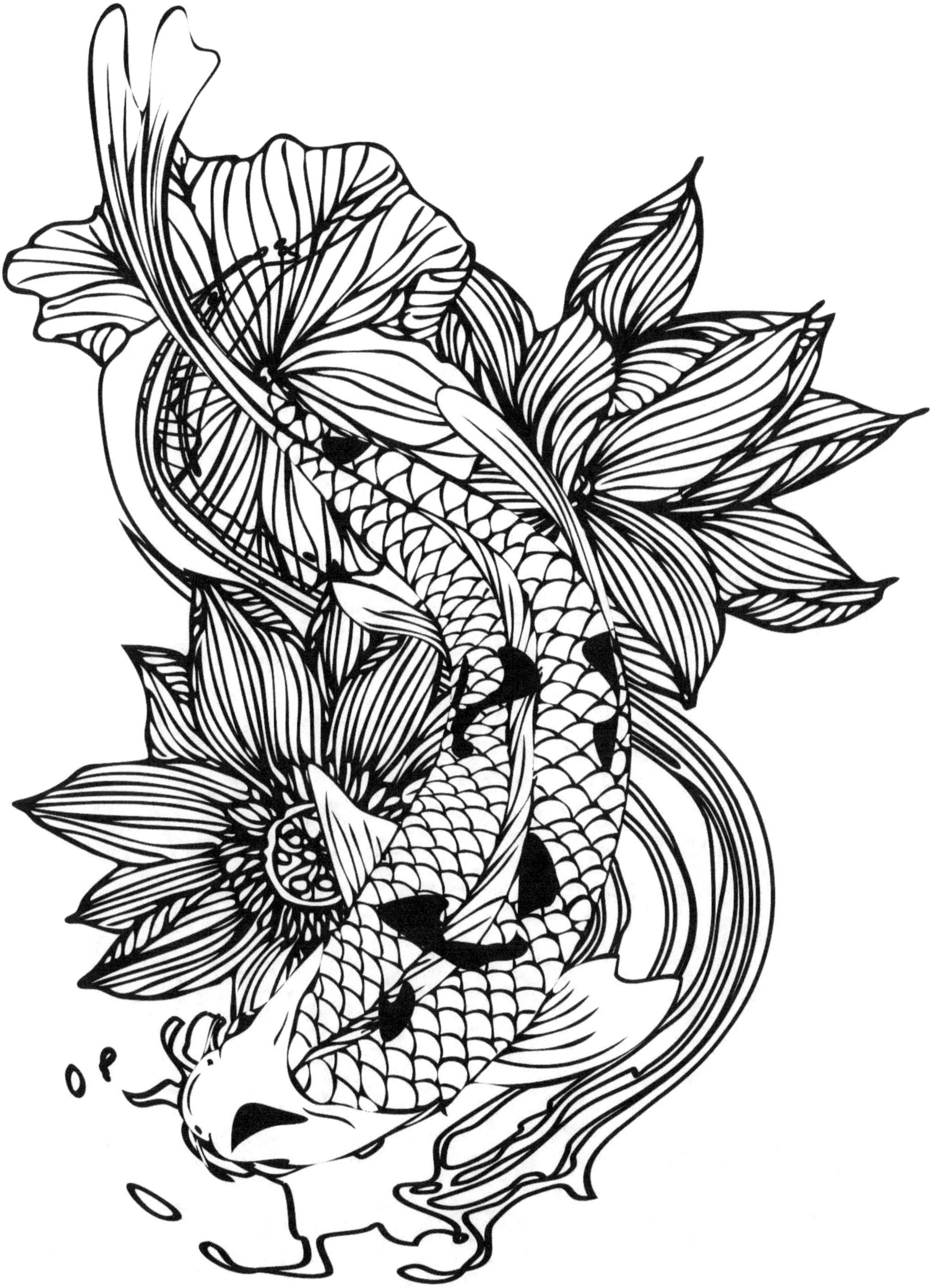

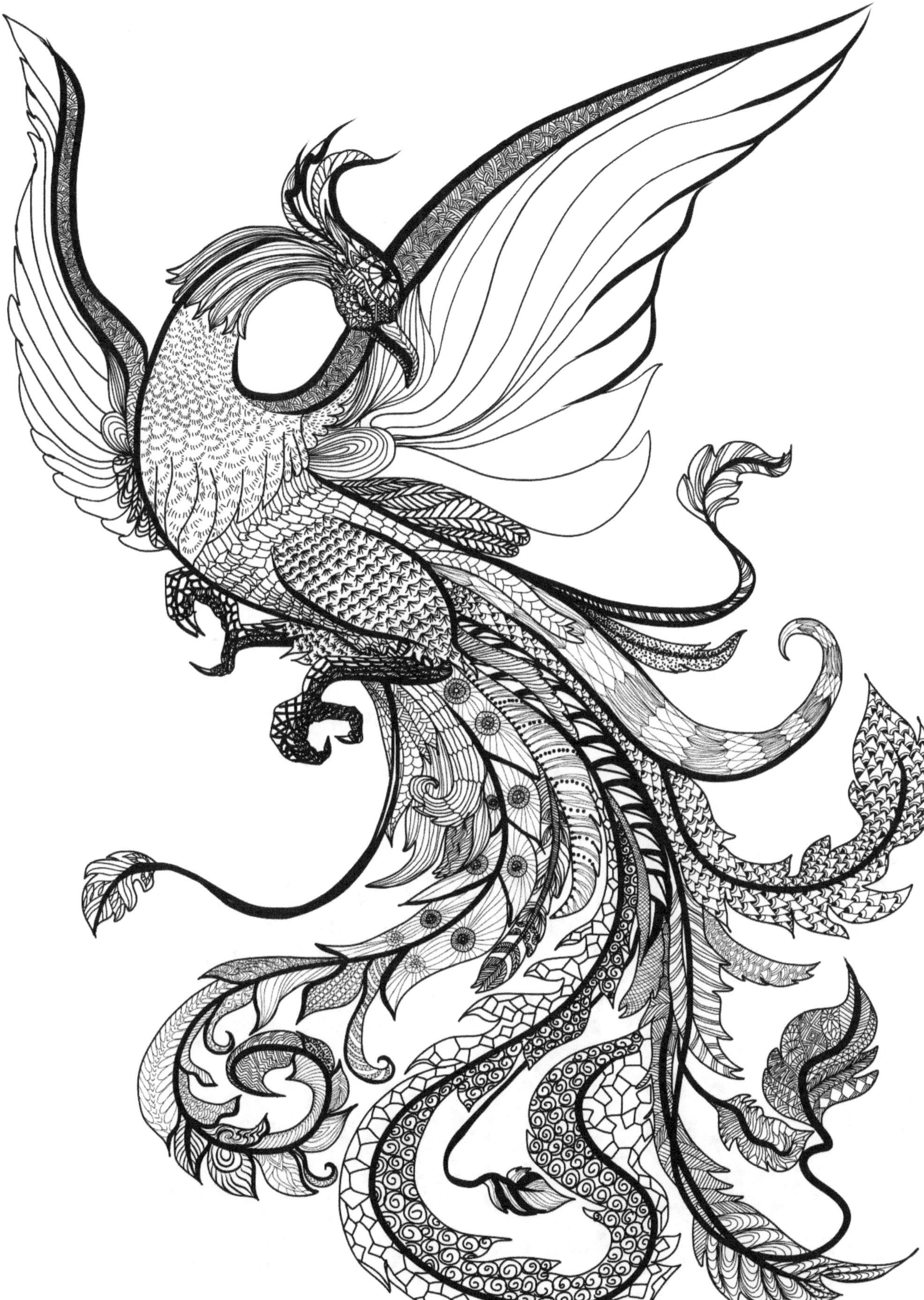

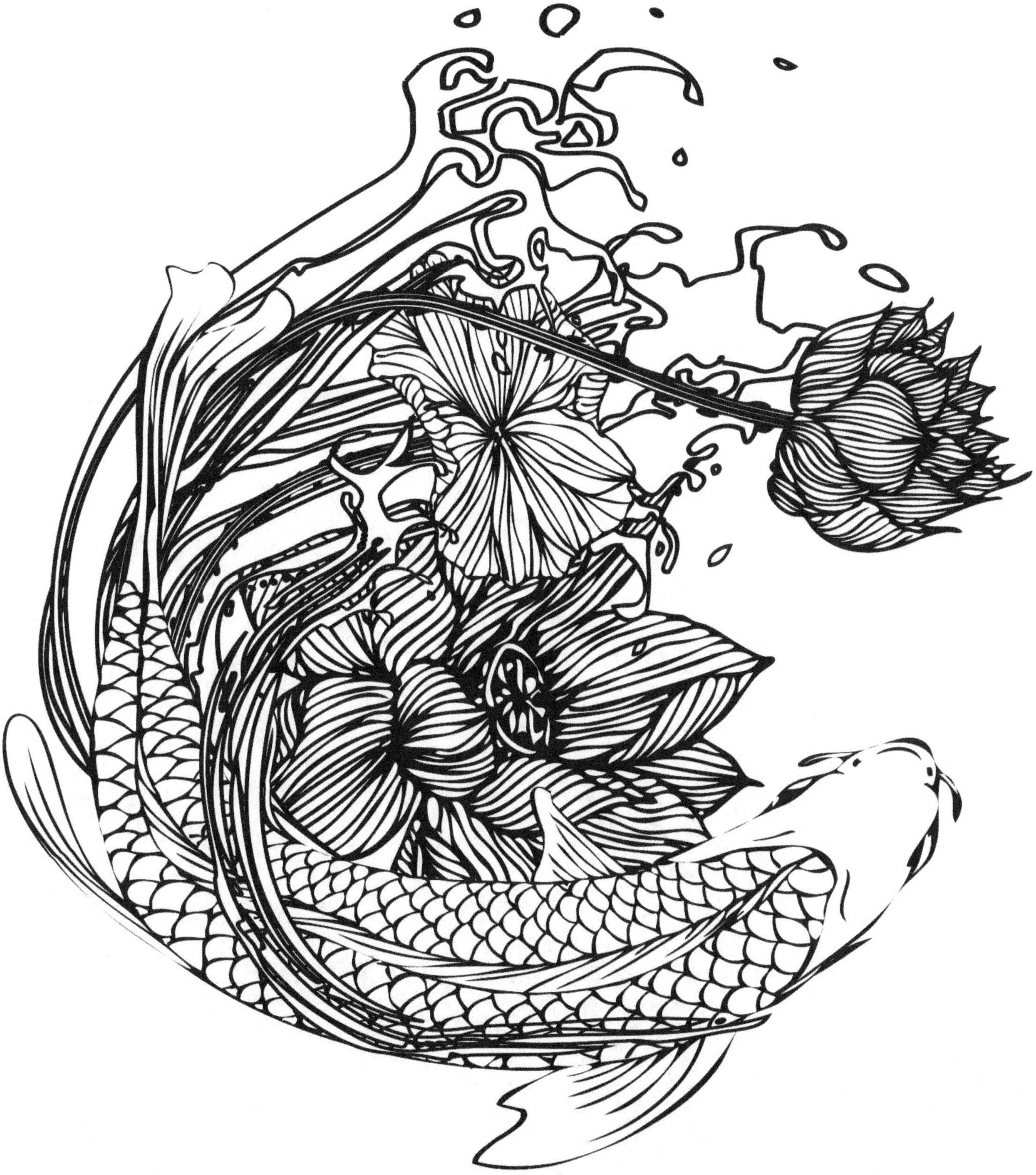

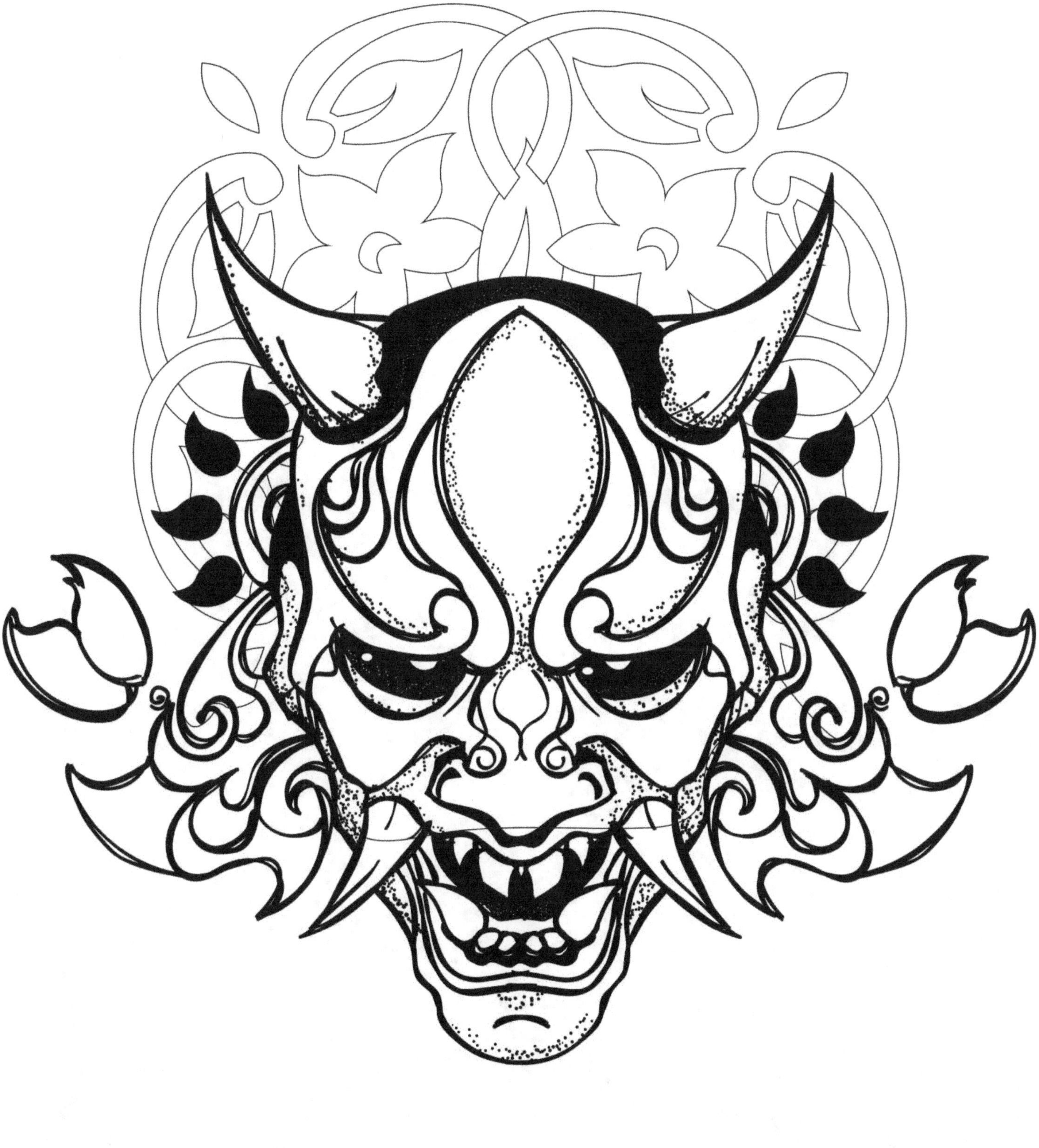

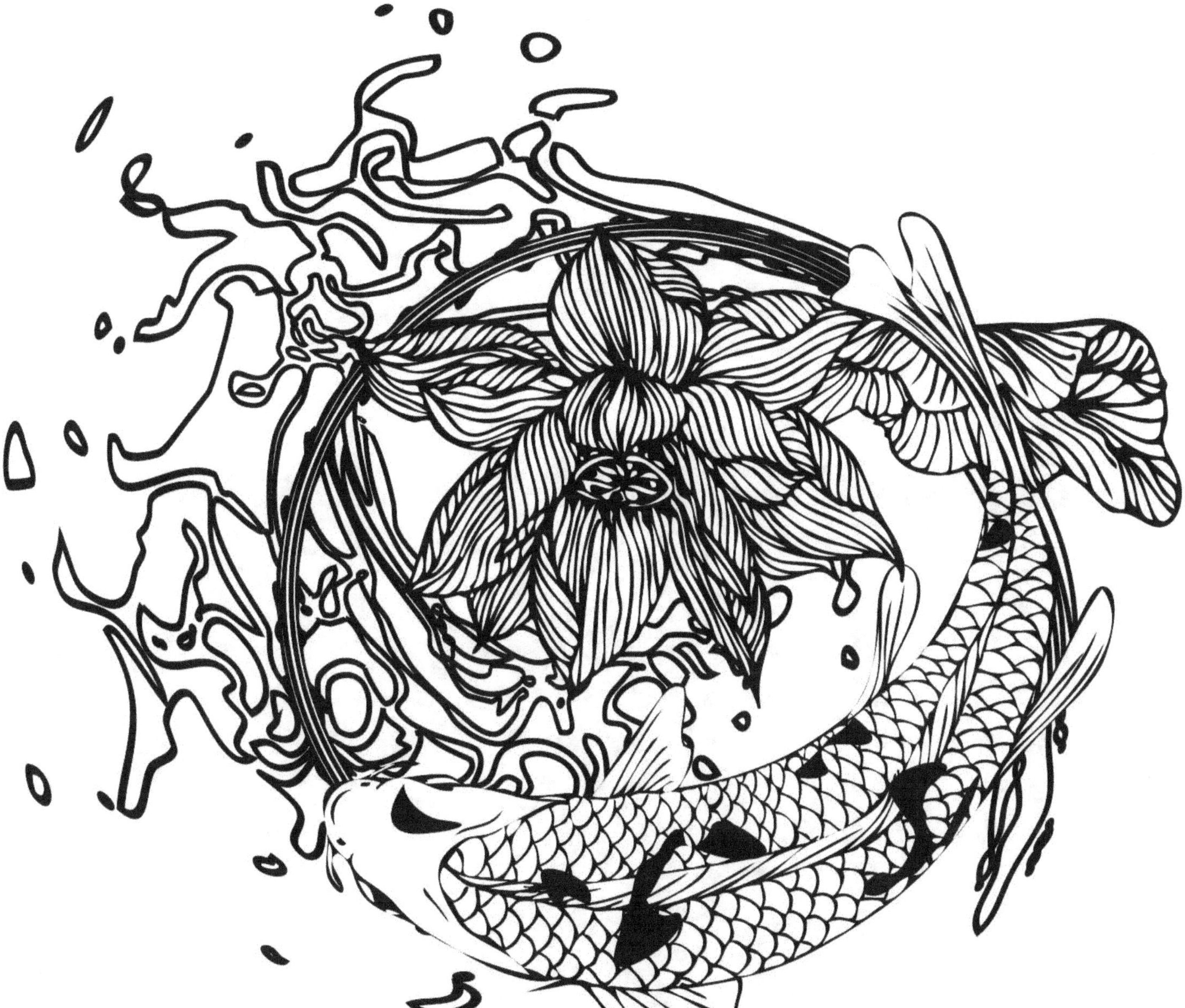

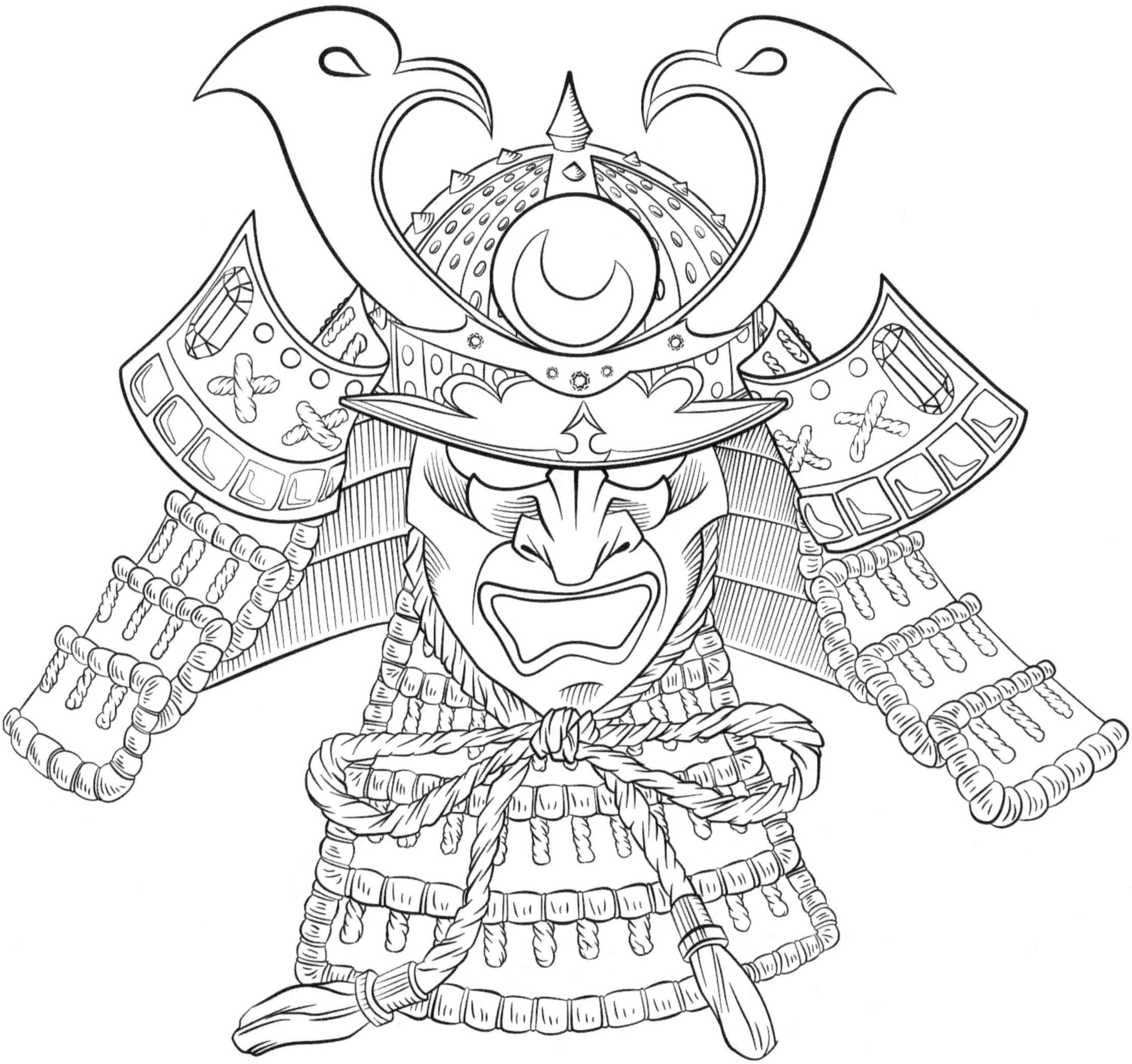

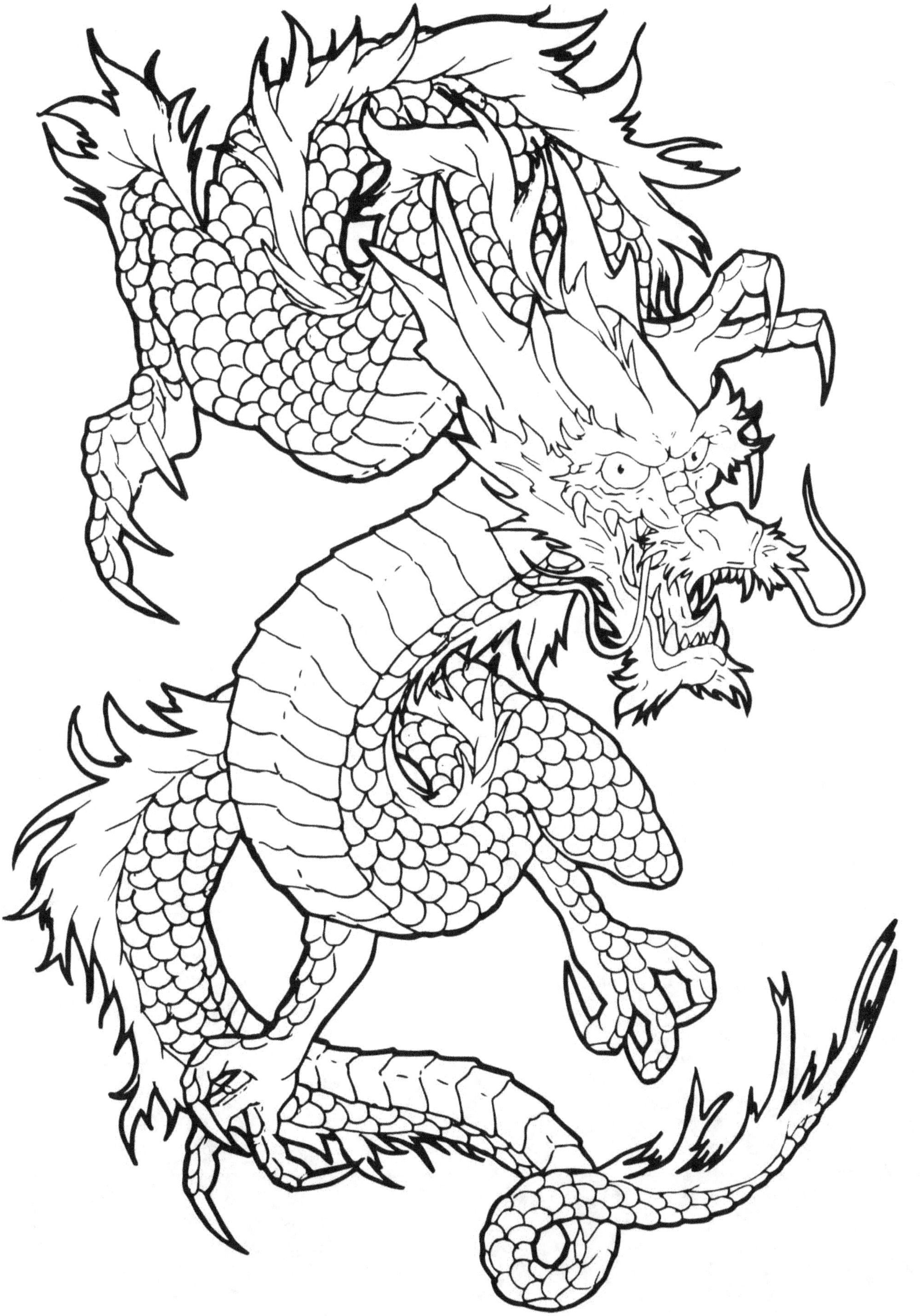

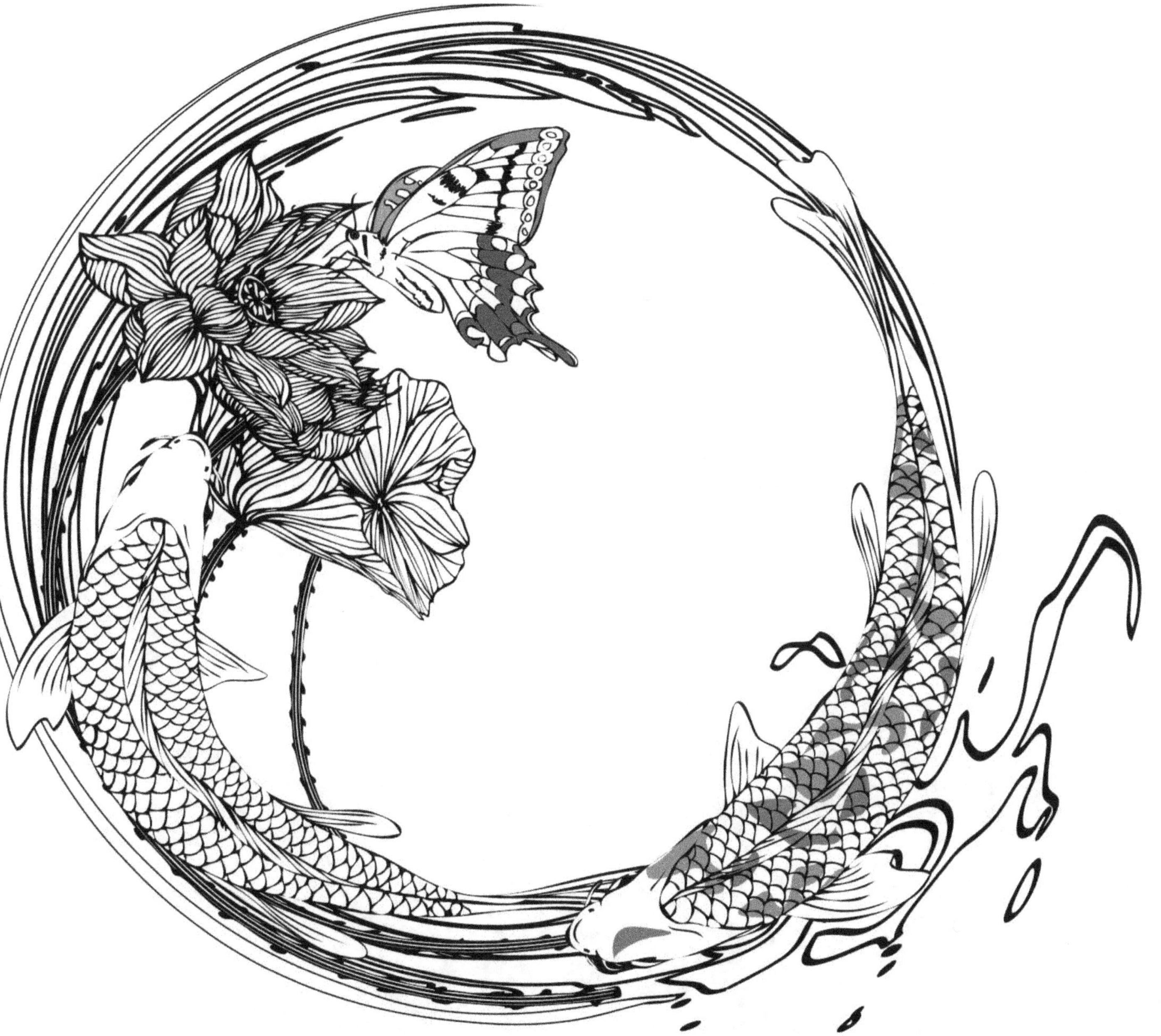

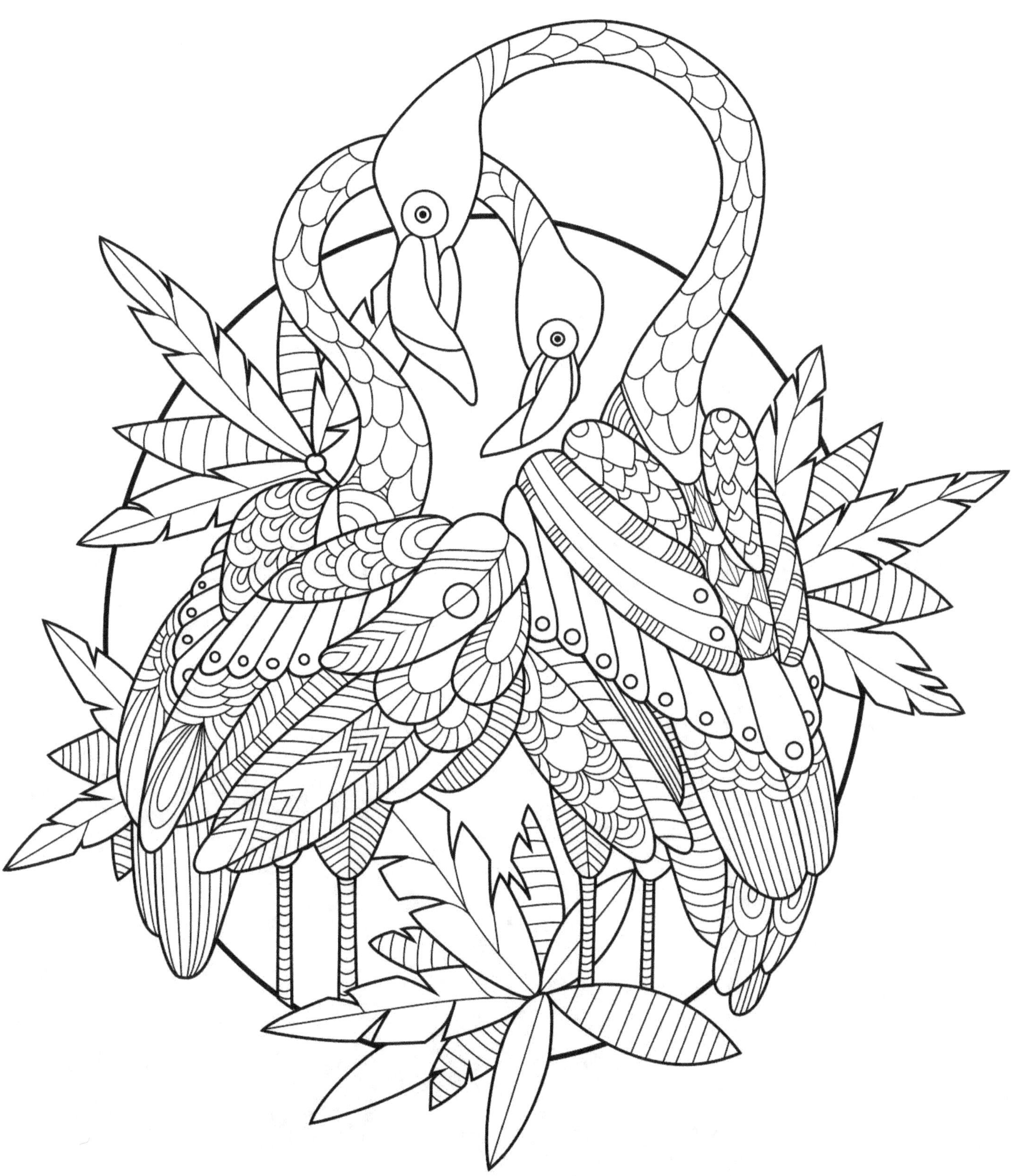

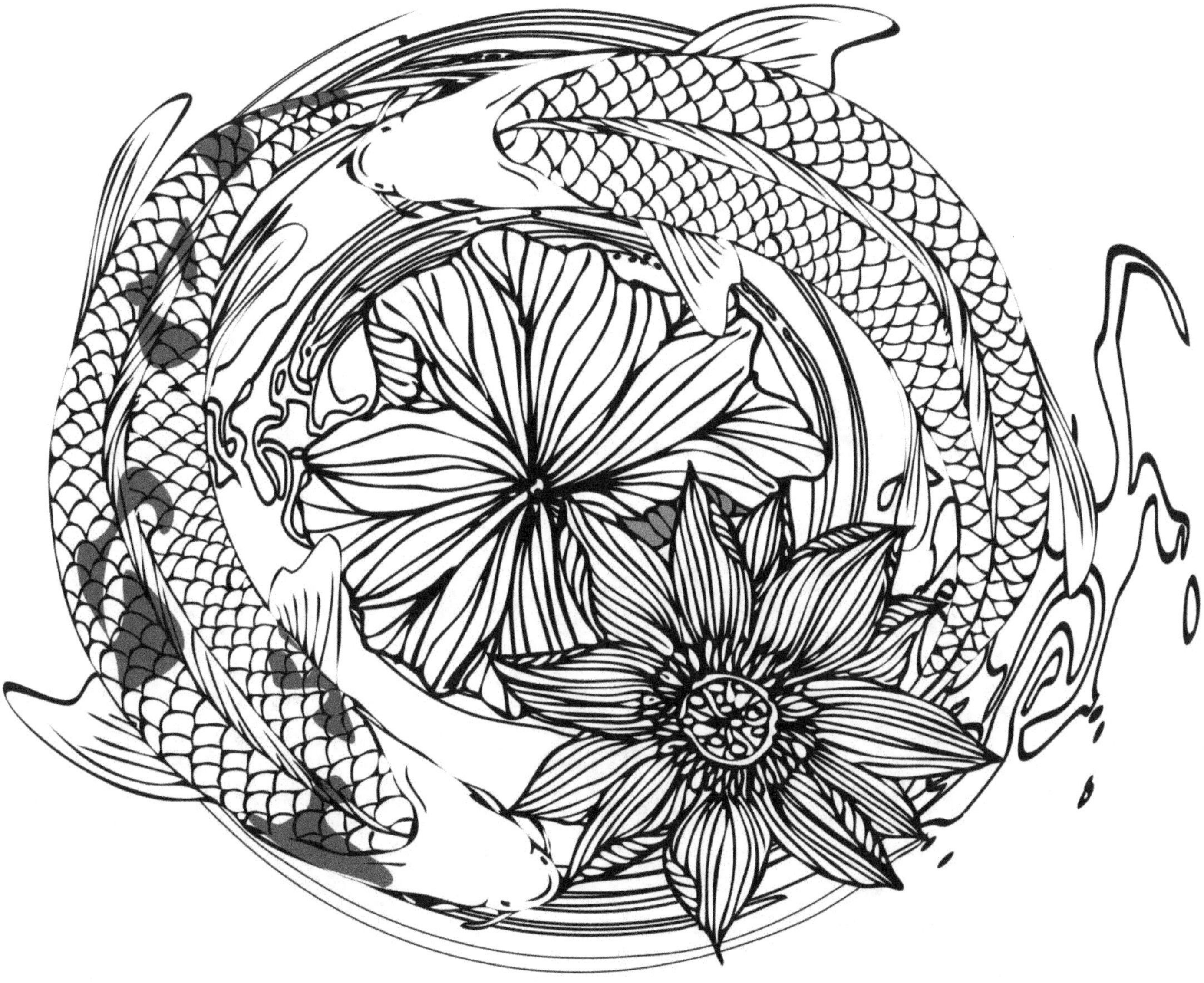

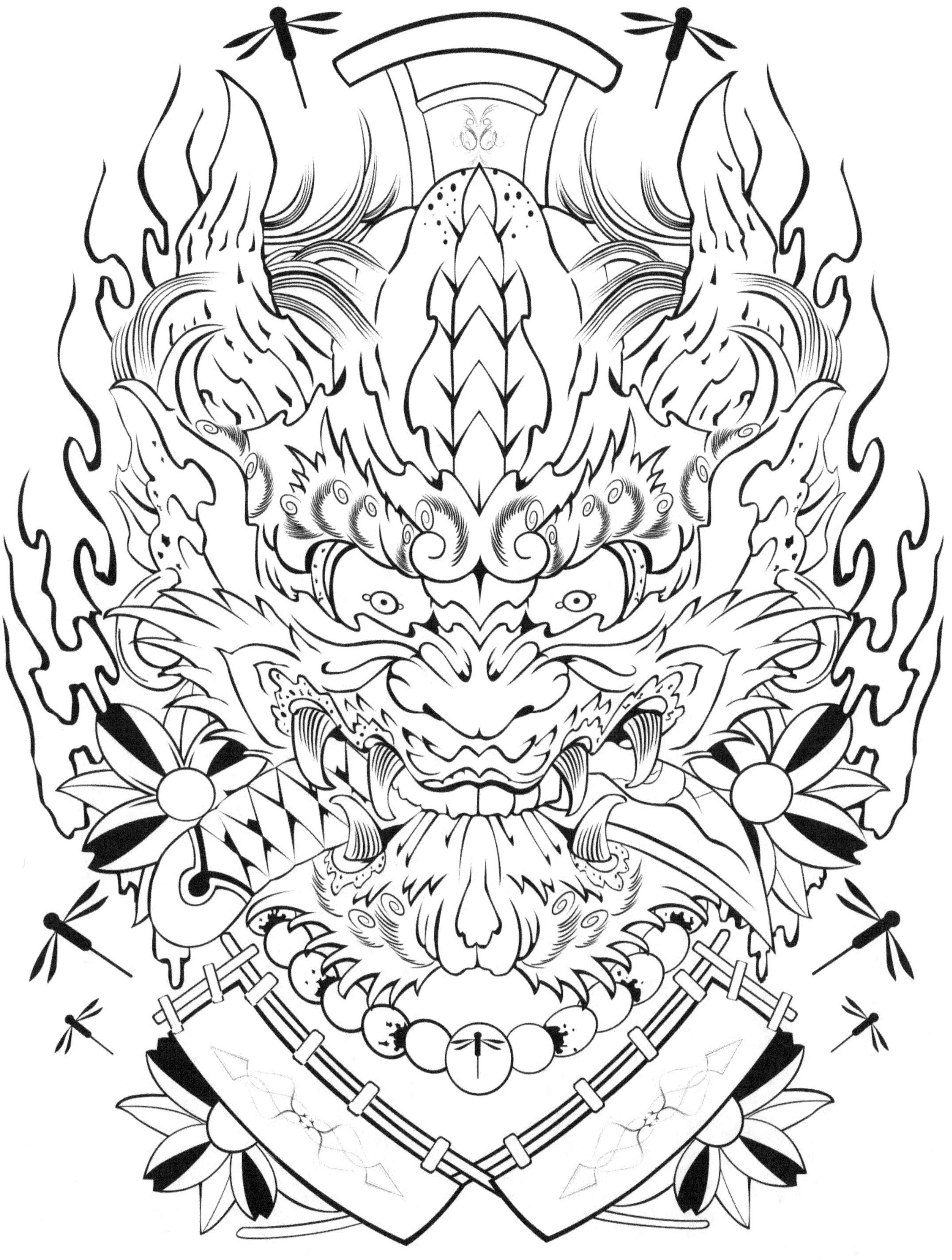

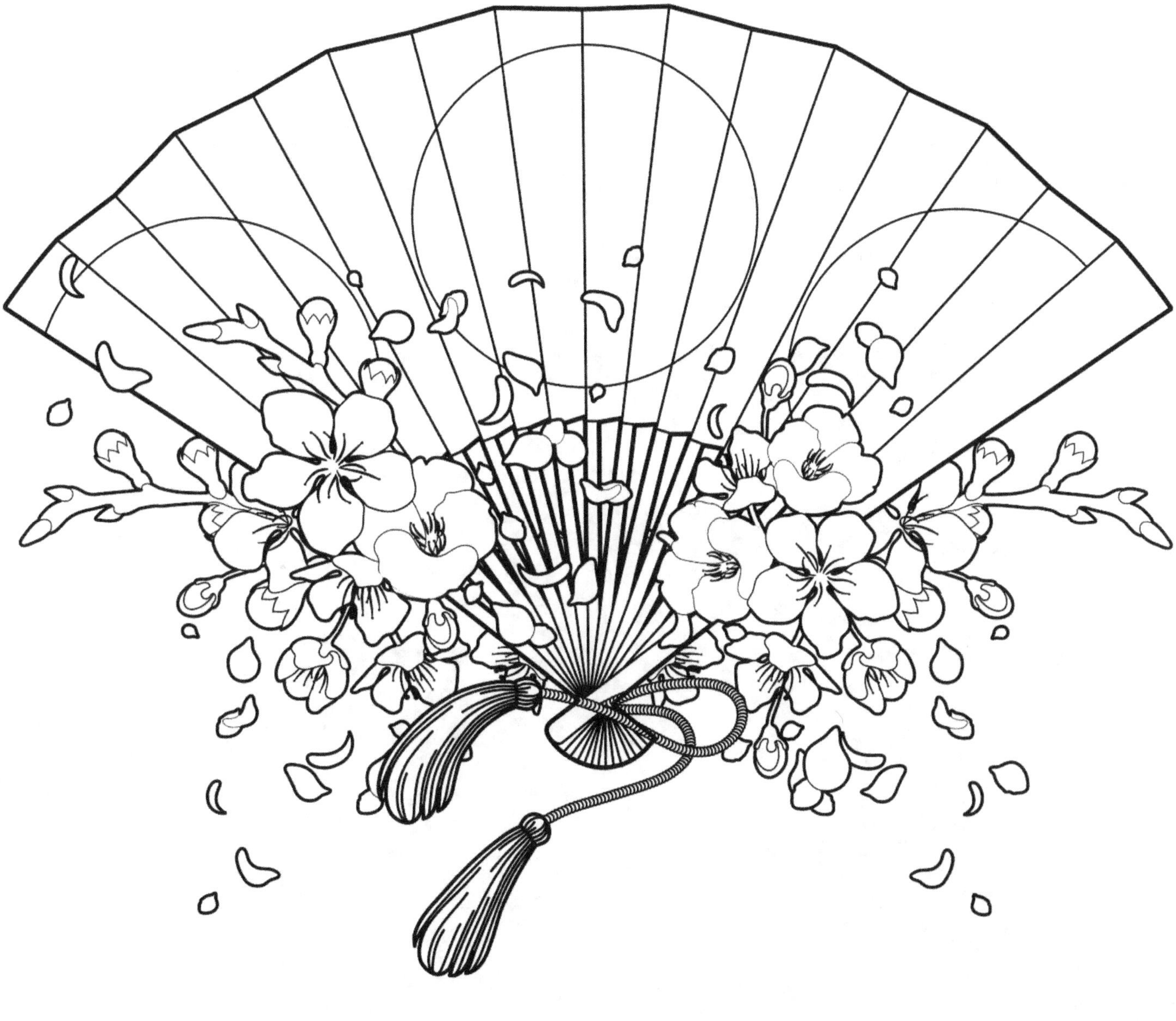

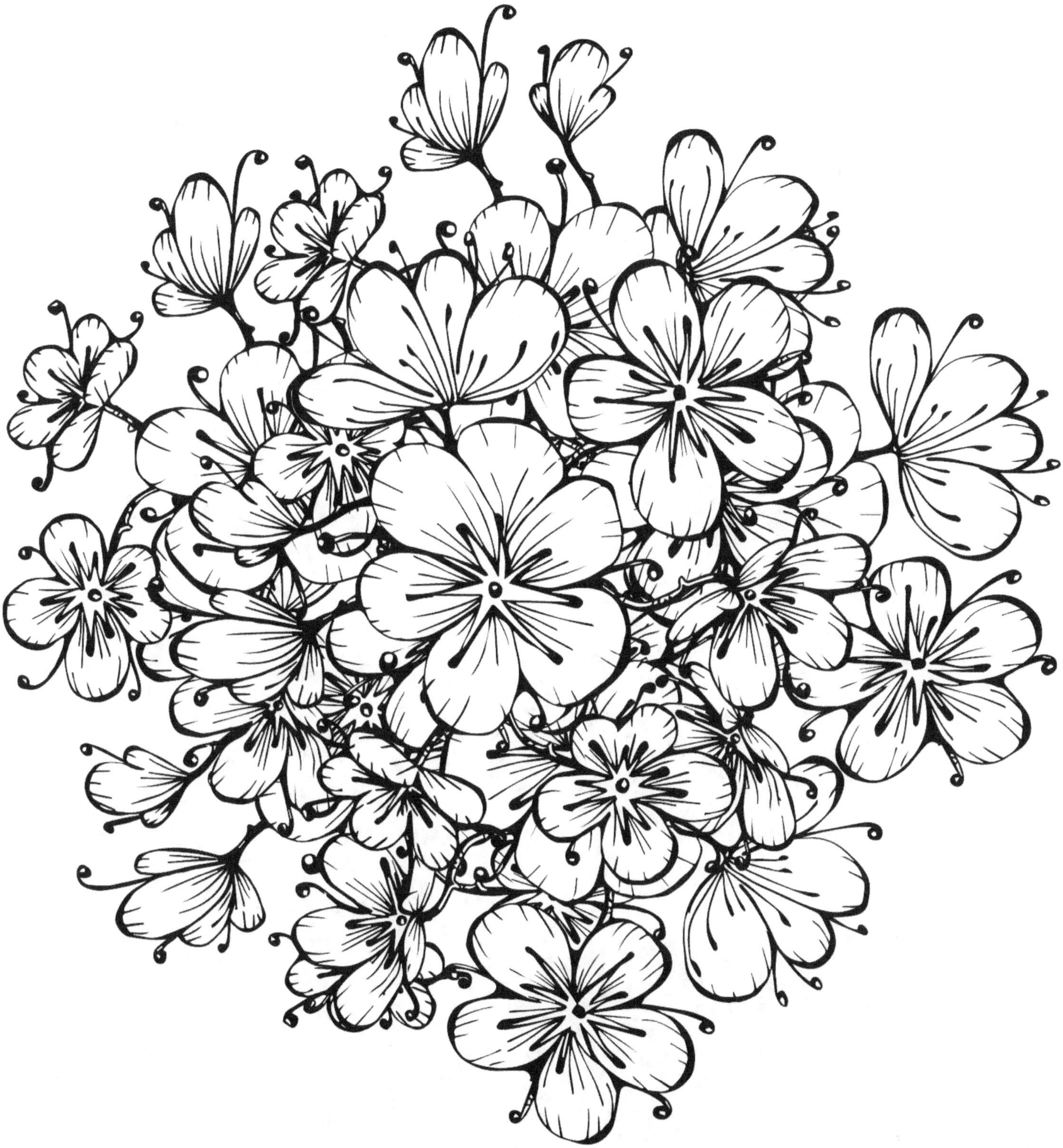

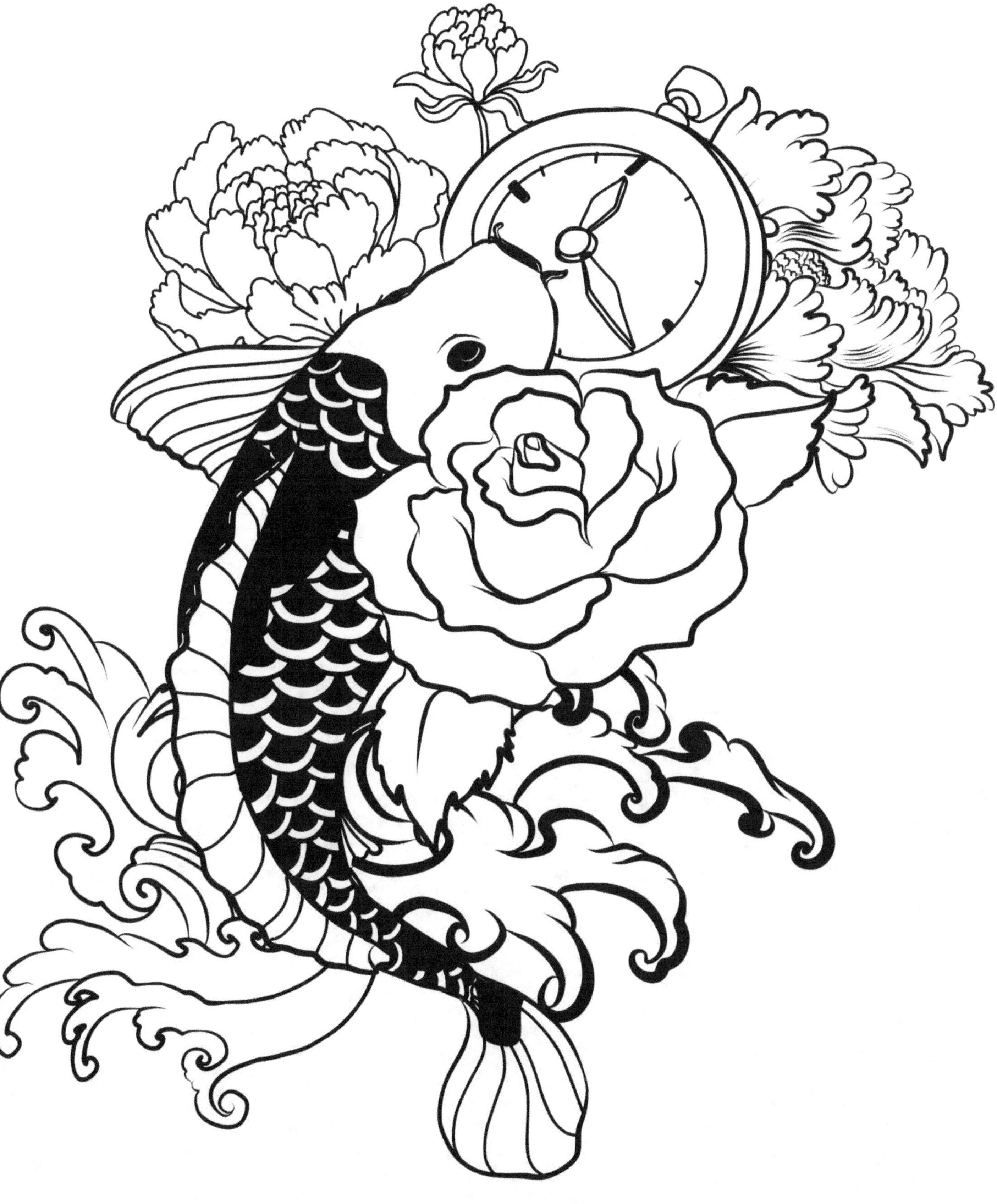

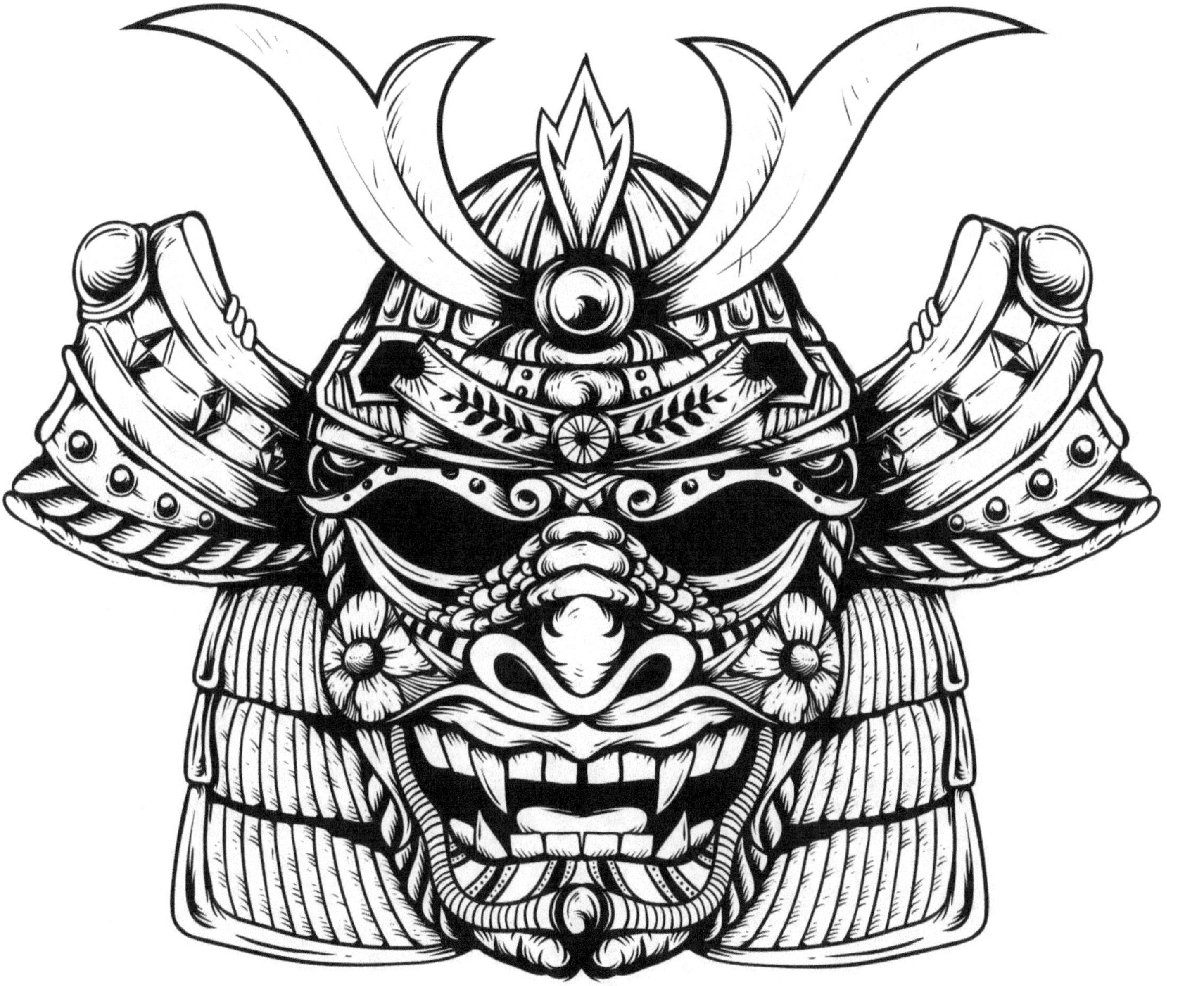

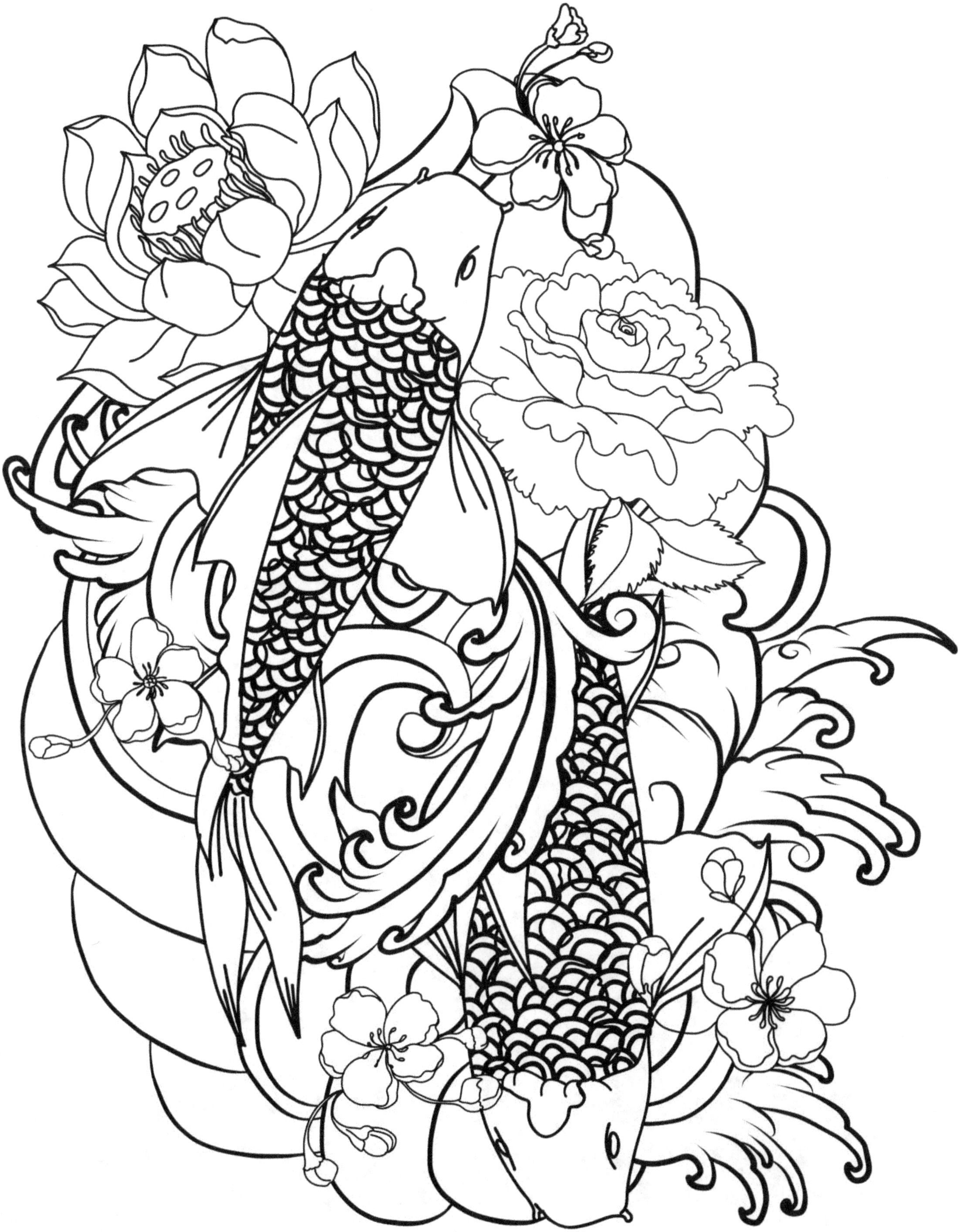

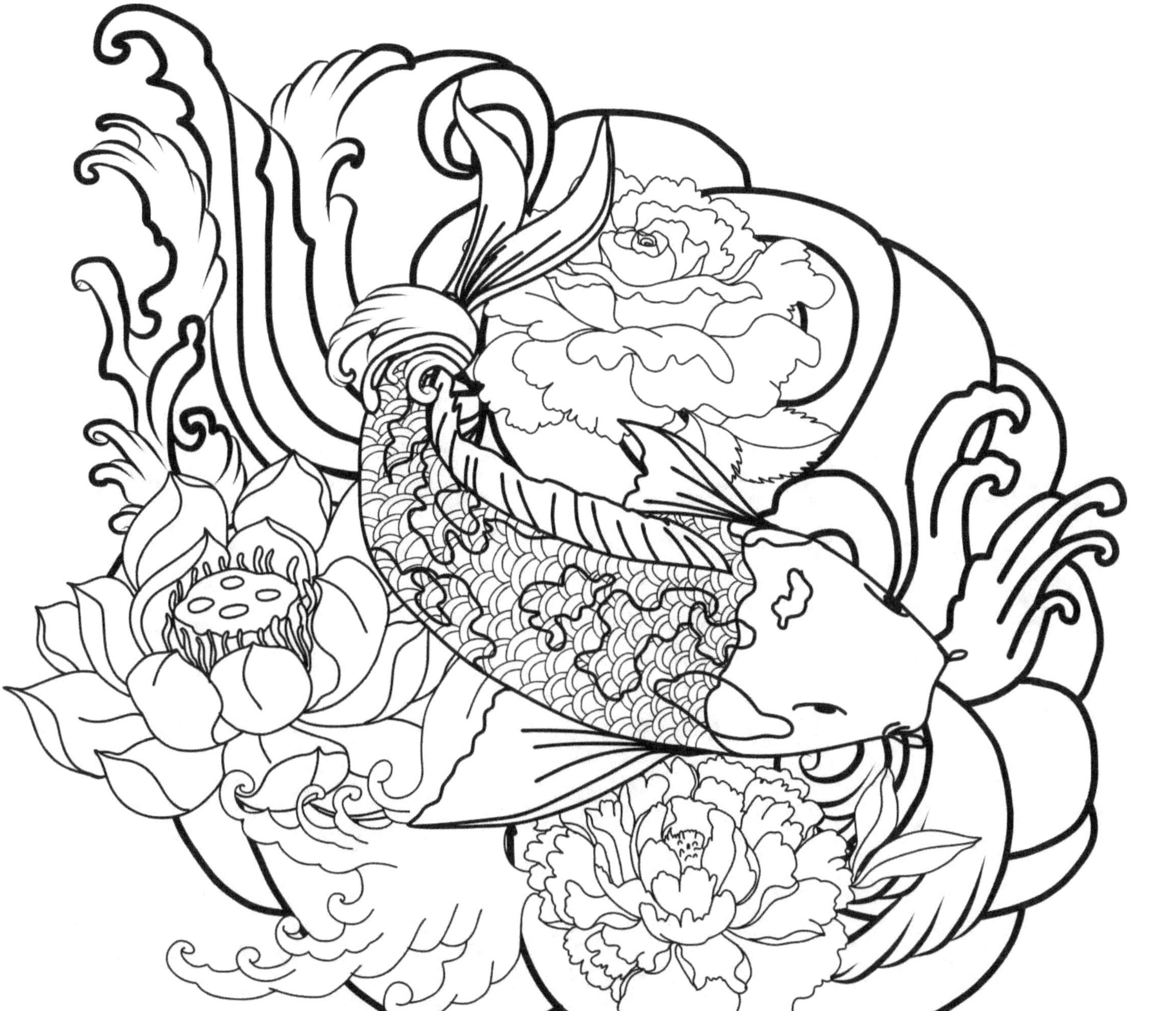

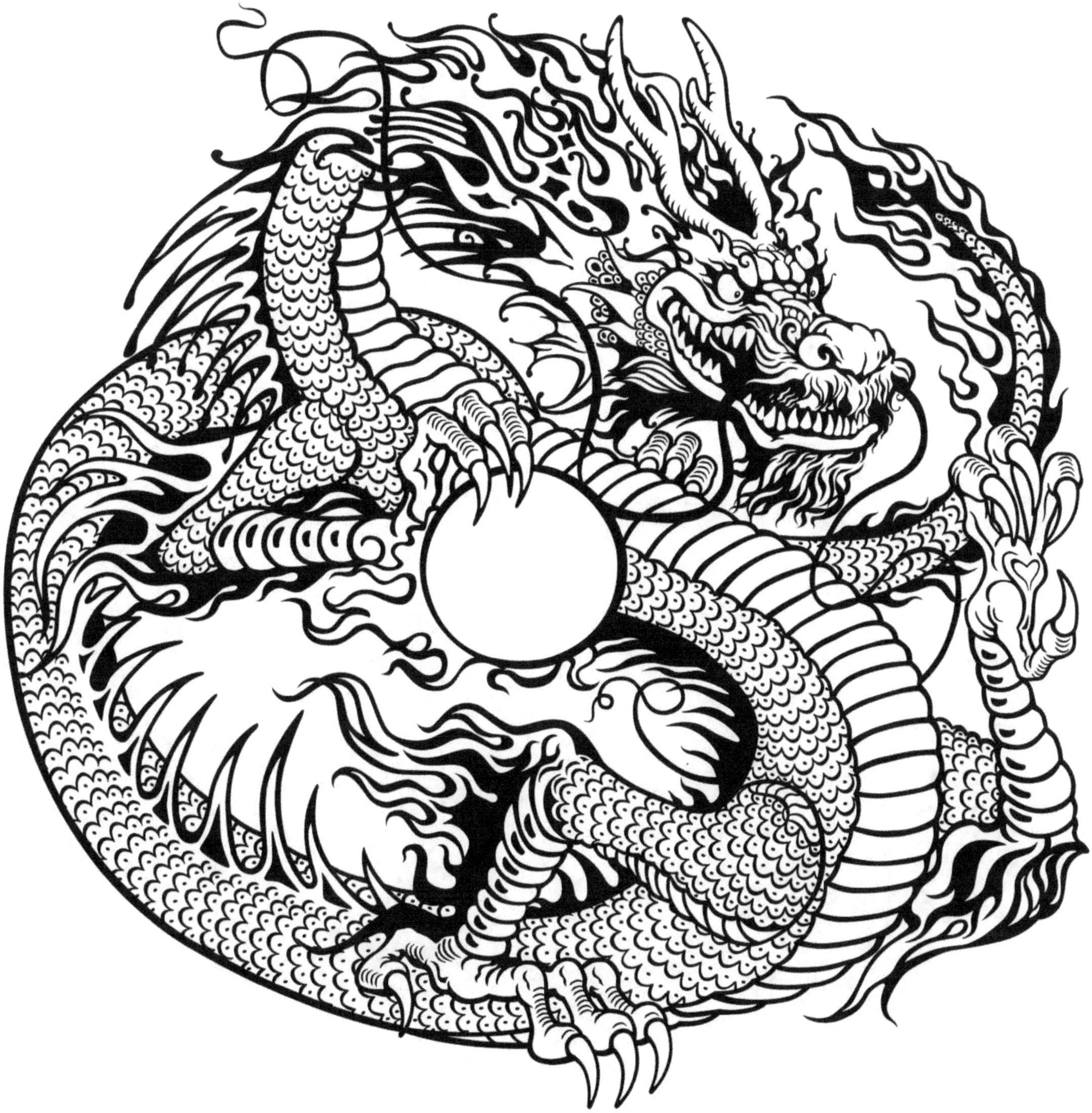

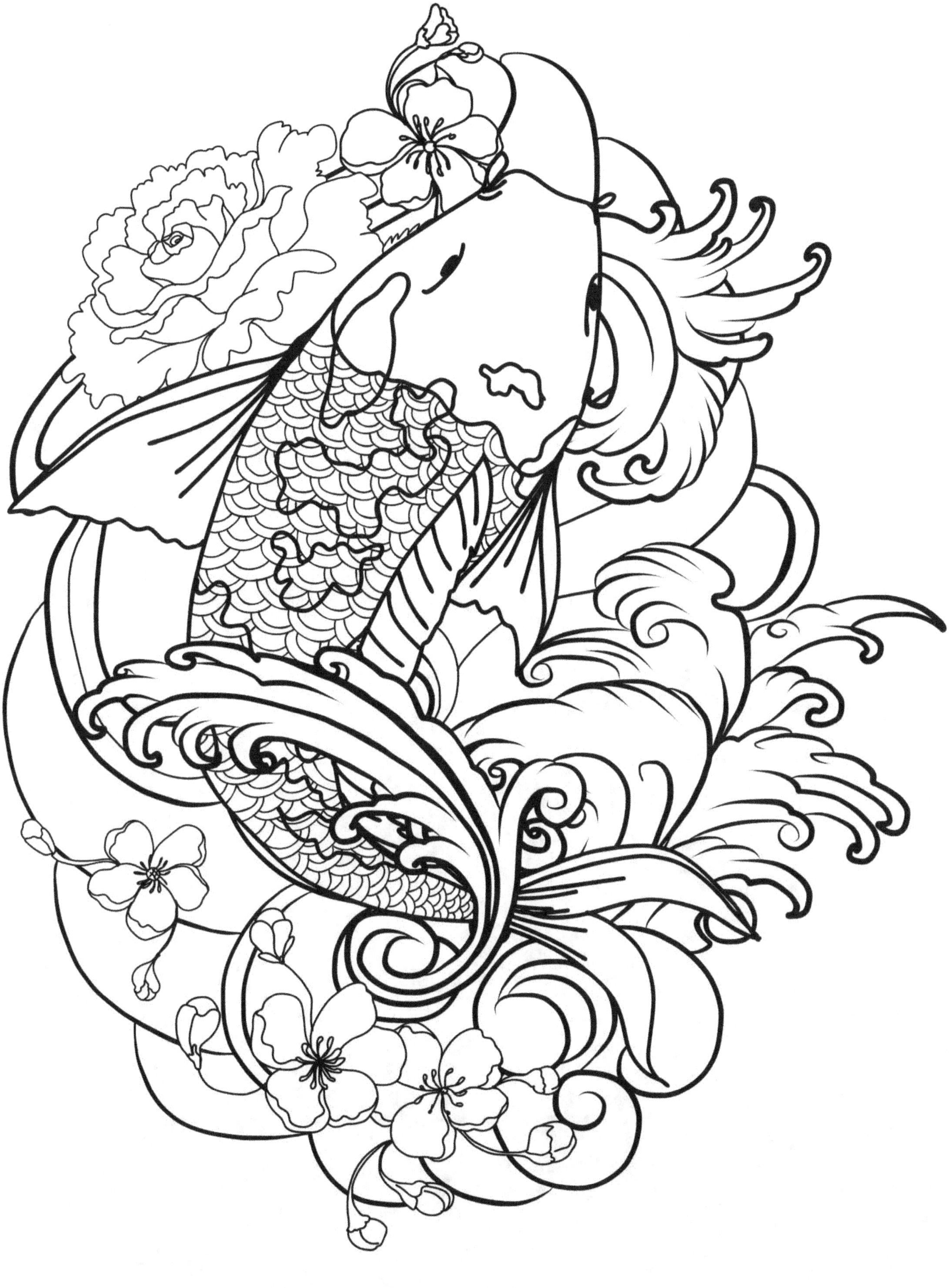

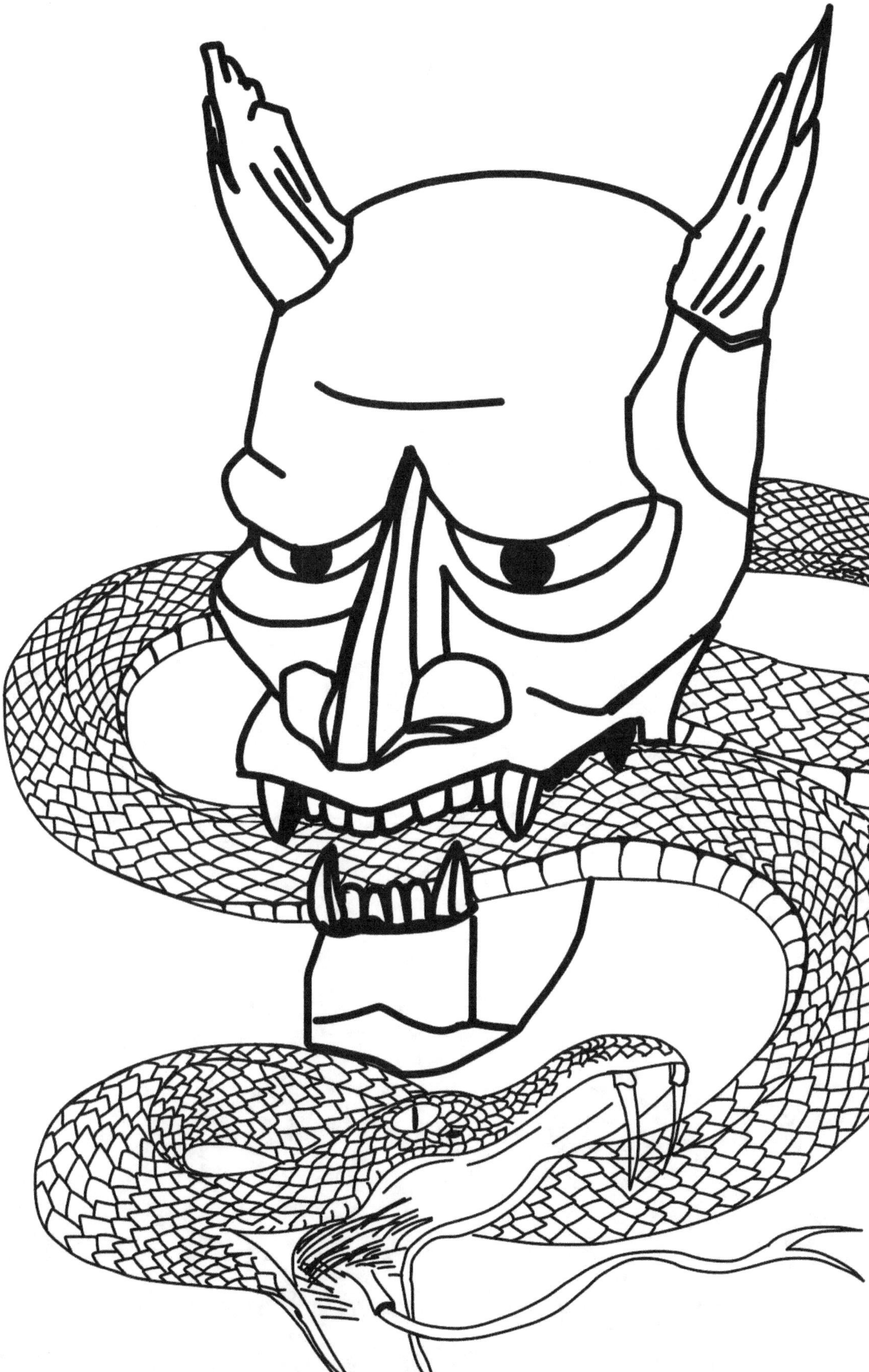

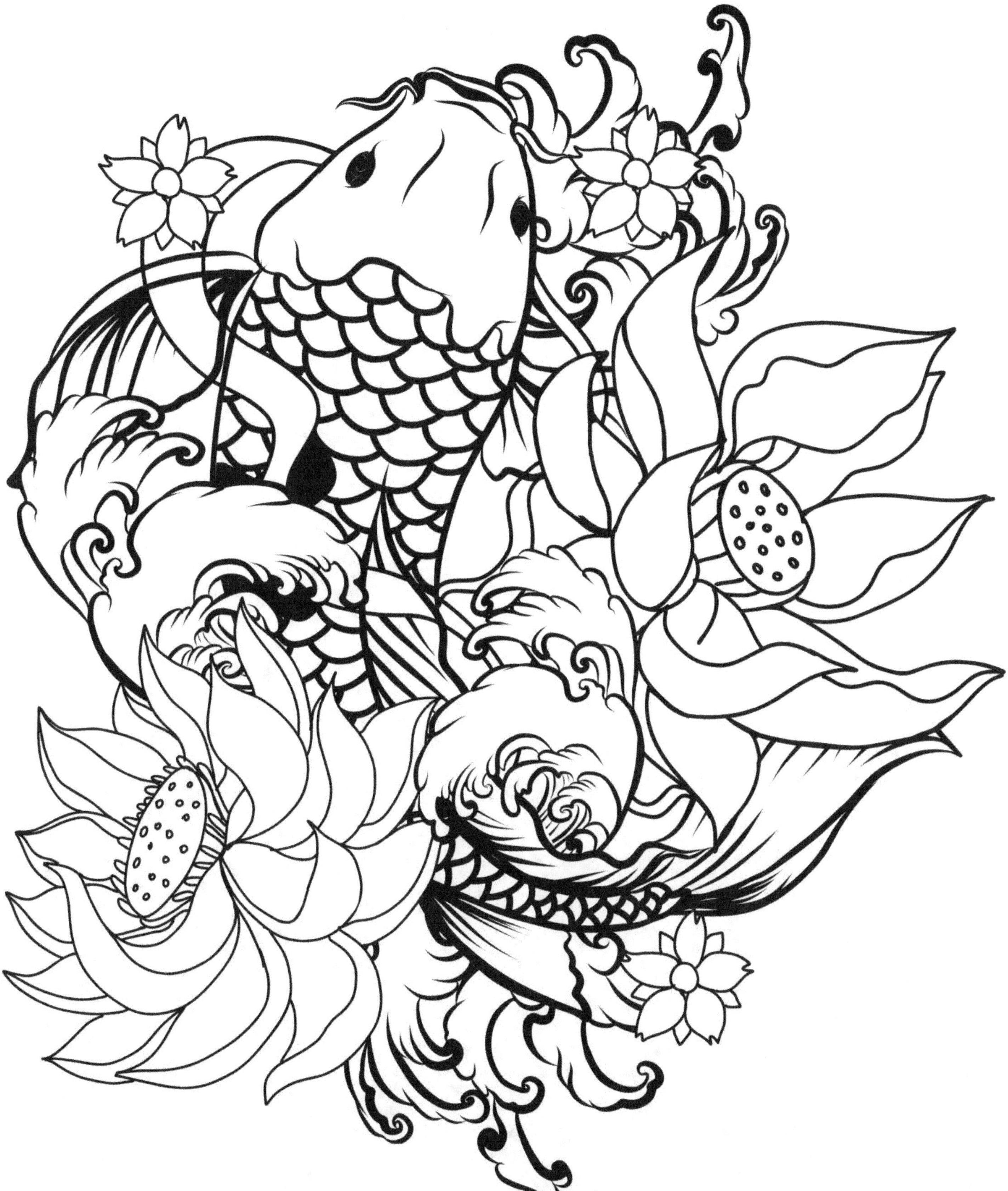

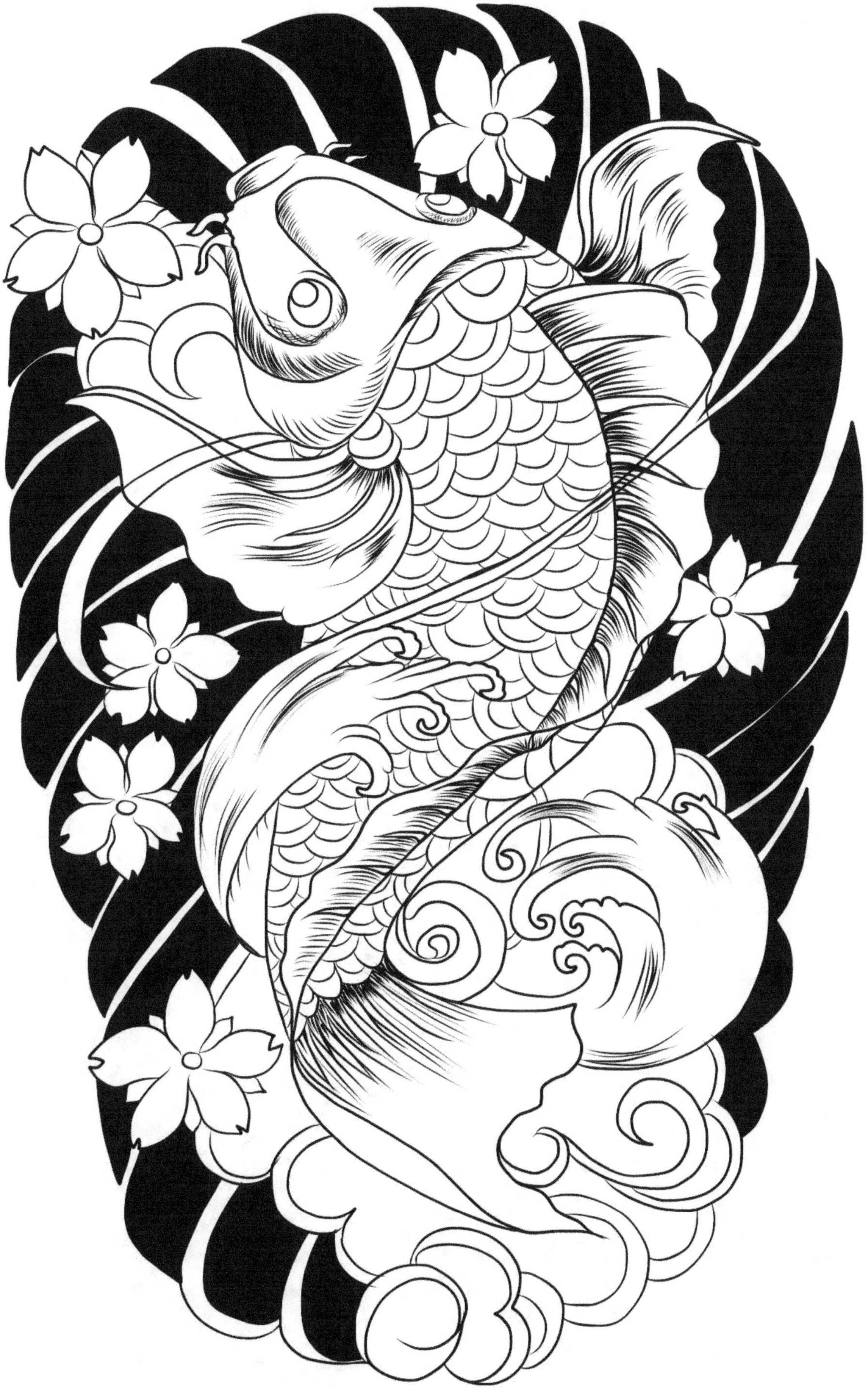

www.ingramcontent.com/pod-product-compliance
Lightning Source LLC
Chambersburg PA
CBHW081901170526
45167CB00007B/3109
* 9 7 8 1 5 4 4 2 0 9 7 3 9 *